Lessons Learned from
Pain's Blessings,
Part 1

and

Sacrifice's Challenges,
Part 2

Lessons Learned from
Pain's Blessings,
Part 1

and

Sacrifice's Challenges,
Part 2

Lydia Samuelson

Ashville, New York
www.painsblessings.com

Copyright © 2010 by Lydia Samuelson.

Edited by Jolene Simmons.

Library of Congress Control Number: 2010908474
ISBN: Softcover   978-1-4535-1782-6

Scripture quotations are taken from the New King James Version. Copyright @ 1979, 1980, 1982, 1994 by Thomas Nelson, Inc.

All rights reserved. No part of this book may be reproduced or transmitted in any form or by any means, electronic or mechanical, including photocopying, recording, or by any information storage and retrieval system, without permission in writing from the copyright owner.

This book was printed in the United States of America.

To order additional copies of this book, contact:
Xlibris Corporation
1-888-795-4274
www.Xlibris.com
Orders@Xlibris.com

Contents

Pain's Blessings
Part One

Dedication		Page ix
Forward		Page xi
Chapter 1	**The New Life**	Page 1
Chapter 2	**The Accident**	Page 3
Chapter 3	**The Recovery**	Page 10
Chapter 4	**The Unexpected Delivery**	Page 13
Chapter 5	**The Blessings Abound**	Page 18
Notes		Page 21
Epilogue		Page 23

Sacrifice's Challenges
Part Two

Dedication		Page iii
Chapter 1	**The Right Opportunity**	Page 1
Chapter 2	**Waiting and Wondering**	Page 6
Chapter 3	**The Sacrifice**	Page 17
Chapter 4	**Discouragement and Hope**	Page 22
Chapter 5	**Perseverance**	Page 27
The Author		Page 31

Pain's Blessings

Part One

To my God and Saviour Who has saved me from fire twice—
from a temporary, earthly fire and from the eternal fire of hell.

Forward

"That I may proclaim with the voice of thanksgiving,
And tell of all Your wondrous works." Psalm 26:7.

Prompted by others to write about my burn accident and the unusual birth of my second son, recognizing the opportunity to fulfill the above verse by sharing this story, wanting to thank people who had helped us after my accident, and burdened to tell people how they can also escape eternal fire and enjoy eternal blessing, I decided that I had to share this story. My prayer is that it will give God glory and help rescue at least one soul from the eternal fire.

Chapter 1

The New Life

It was early January 2002. My husband Jeff, my only son Judah, and I were visiting my brother Dan and his family in Clarks Summit, Pennsylvania, about five hours from our country home snuggled in the far western corner of New York. Although I enjoyed our visit, I felt unusually tired and kept smelling a putrid odor that no one else noticed. I guessed why I was having these symptoms, but told no one else yet. After we returned home, the strange symptoms seemed to disappear until about a week and a half later when I began to feel sick and only felt better when I ate more. I then took a home pregnancy test and confirmed my original suspicions; I was pregnant. I responded with mixed emotions. For eight years we had been unable to have another baby. In 2001, I had prayed daily for a second child and was excited to realize now that God had answered this prayer. At the same time, I felt confused. Jeff was hoping to go to school for full-time ministry, and I, therefore, was intending to search for full-time work. Now I didn't know what would happen, or how Jeff would react. But he humbly accepted the announcement of another baby as God's will for him not to go to school for ministry at that time.

I should have been rejoicing because of the blessing of finally having another baby on the way, but during my first trimester I was too sick to care. This sickness was the first of several ways during the year of 2002 that I was going to experience one of life's most important lessons—blessings do not come without pain and problems. A farmer experiences this lesson every year as he first must toil hard planting and then spend weeks patiently waiting before he can finally reap a bountiful harvest. A marathon runner willingly accepts this lesson while painfully training hard for months and then enduring 26.2 grueling miles of running in order to triumphantly cross the finish line. Jesus chose to learn this lesson when He "for the joy that was set before Him endured the cross,"(Hebrews 12:2) so that He might redeem for Himself a spotless bride (see note #1). While going through a painful struggle, it is hard to imagine the joy ahead of us. Sometimes we don't feel like going on, and need to remind ourselves that he who endures to the end will be blessed. I was going to learn to appreciate pain's blessings more than once during 2002

During the first trimester of this pregnancy, I truly felt so sick that I wondered how I would be able to endure nine months of such agony! I was too sick to cook for anyone and couldn't even fix my own food; I only left the house twice a week—once on Sunday to teach Sunday School and another time to help clean my church; I couldn't drive; and I often just sat on my couch feeling like a zombie. Finally, one morning toward the end of March during my daily walk, I noticed that I did not feel as sick as usual. When I returned home, I told Jeff and Judah, "I actually felt well enough to enjoy my walk today." From then on I continued to grow stronger. At last, I was able to look back on my first trimester and appreciate the blessing of having family and friends who had so willingly helped me while I felt so sick, doing such activities for me as driving, cooking, and grocery shopping.

But soon another unpleasant trial began. I developed a swollen varicose vein that made it very painful to walk. Jeff and I had chosen to use a midwife rather than a regular doctor for this pregnancy. The midwife recommended an herbal product called Vari-Gone from Nature's Sunshine Products, Inc. that improves circulation and helps maintain healthy veins. This product alone greatly helped relieve the agony of the swollen vein.

Finally, toward the end of April, I was feeling well enough to become more active outside my home. I offered to substitute at our local public school. I had been a teacher before Judah was born, but now was only home schooling Judah and doing some tutoring. My first opportunity to substitute was for the afternoon of Thursday, April 25, 2002. Being aware of the day's hectic schedule, I tried to plan accordingly, but was totally unprepared for all the events that would transpire.

In the morning I taught Judah and tutored a girl at my home. Then, taking Judah along, I zoomed thirteen miles to Chautauqua Lake Central School to substitute. After school, I returned home, picked up my eleven-year-old niece, Amber, who lived next door, and took her and Judah back up toward the school to go swimming at a physical fitness center. I had decided to swim some days rather than walk or run to relieve the pressure on the swollen varicose vein. After swimming, I rushed home to do the animal chores. We lived in a trailer on my father's farm. Although my father no longer had any farm animals, we had goats and chickens.

Chapter 2

The Accident

    Finally around 8:00 P.M., I settled into my small kitchen to begin supper. Jeff was not home yet, but Judah and I were famished! I had planned a simple meal of cream beef over bread. I turned on the gas stove to heat the beef, but the burner did not light. We were having trouble with our stovetop lighting consistently. So I bent down to blow on the burner to start the flame. I was talking on the phone at the same time to my neighbor Lisa and turned my head just as the burner lit. A large flame flared up, catching the long hair of the left side of my head on fire. I yelled into the phone, "Just a minute, I'm on fire!" I threw down the phone and immediately thrust my head under the kitchen faucet, which was right by the stove. I began to panic when I couldn't douse the fire quickly.

    Terrified as I watched my hair burn up in flames, I thought of hell. Though the fire was scary, I was grateful that it was only temporary and that I would never have to experience the eternal flames of hell because I know the Lord Jesus Christ as my Savior (see note # 2).

    Judah and Amber were sitting on the couch in our living room. Since the living room is just a larger extension of the kitchen, they were able to observe the whole episode of my hair shooting up in flames. When I yelled for help, Amber jumped up and grabbed a jug from my refrigerator. In her haste, she did not realize that it was a jug of milk, not water. But she never had to use it because I had finally put out the fire. Lisa called back to check on me. Not knowing the extent of my burn, I said that I was okay. Ironically, Lisa is a nurse, and she told me later that she would have come up immediately to help if she had known how badly burned I was (she lives only about three-quarters of a mile down the road).

Although I could feel some pain, it was not enough to concern me yet. I was more worried about cleaning up the stinky burned hair and about how much hair I would have to get cut to make it all look even. I asked Amber to call her Mom, my oldest sister Melita, who still lived with my parents next door, to ask her to run over and help me clean up the mess. When her mom did not answer, Amber and Judah ran next door to the old farmhouse to get her. In the meantime, I traipsed down our narrow hallway to the bathroom to better clean off the burned hair. Looking into the mirror, I noticed a white streak running down the left side of my neck and for the first time became concerned that my burn may be more serious than I had first thought. When Melita arrived, I asked her what she thought about the extent of the burn. We decided to call our neighbor Randy, a volunteer fireman who lived about three-quarters of a mile up the road. I assumed that he would be able to tell me how to treat the burn or, at most, suggest that I go to the emergency room for a little more extensive care. Melita called Randy while I continued to clean off the burned hair in my tiny bathroom's sink.

During this time, Amber was trying to contact Jeff. She got no answer on his cell phone, but then she saw him drive into my parents' driveway where he parked his work truck by my father's barn. Melita ran up to the barn to tell Jeff about my accident.

Randy came over promptly after Melita's phone call to help me. He informed me that I was doing the best thing by dousing my head under water (although I had just been trying to deal with the burned hair, I was also getting needed water on the burned skin). He wrapped my head in a cold, wet towel; had me sit on the living room couch; and then, to my amazement, called 9-1-1! Soon my little trailer was swarming with firemen and other medical assistants. I was baffled by all the fuss. When we were told that I needed to go in an ambulance to the hospital, Jeff voiced my thoughts, "Does she need to go by ambulance? Can't I just take her?" We were told "no."

Throughout all the commotion, I was concerned about Judah and Amber, who had seen the accident and were still in the living room while the emergency crew was examining me. But the children remained calm and helped whenever asked.

When the ambulance arrived, I felt awkward to be carried by stretcher to it since I was perfectly capable of walking. Jeff and I had decided to have me taken to Westfield Memorial Hospital, about forty-five minutes from our home. So when the ambulance turned right out of my driveway instead of left, the direction we would take to go to Westfield, I was confused. But I was told that we were going to meet an EMT coming from a different direction. Less than five minutes from my house, shortly before the nurse Lisa's house, we met the EMT. I became confused again when we remained sitting along the edge of the road for several more minutes even after the EMT had joined us. The ambulance crew explained that they were waiting to hear from the Westfield hospital as to whether or not they considered themselves equipped enough to take a badly burned patient. Finally, the hospital contacted the ambulance—they decided to take me because the EMT had concluded that I had only first-degree burns. The EMT's diagnosis only confirmed my uncomfortable feeling about so much attention being made about my burn. I was also becoming very concerned about finances since I have no health insurance.

When we arrived at Westfield, I was immediately taken into the emergency room. The nurses first checked the baby's heartbeat. I was relieved that it was normal. Then the nurses began to pour ice water over the left side of my head and neck. Shivering, I tried to remain cheerful. I perked up when I saw that the doctor on call was my own personal doctor who had delivered Judah—Dr. Mark Hagen. He gently touched the burned area of the left side of my head and neck in several spots asking if it hurt. I told him, "no," assuming that I felt no pain because I was slightly burned and again felt embarrassed to even be there. Imagine my shock then when he informed me that they were sending me to the special burn unit at Erie County Medical Center (ECMC) in Buffalo, New York, at least an hour and a half from our home in Ashville. Finally I realized that I had not been feeling major pain because so many nerves had been destroyed by third-degree burns! Now, realizing that my burns were going to require more serious treatment than I had imagined, I became extremely concerned about finances. But God was my comfort.

Jeff then arrived with our pastor, Reverend Charlie Colton. They cheered me up as they laughed at me shivering from the ice water dousing. (I figured that I would surely catch a cold from such chilly treatment, and I did get one in the hospital.) We also joked that I would have to borrow Pastor's hilarious costume wig after I got out of the hospital until my hair grew back. (Pastor Colton was a real comedian and sometimes appeared in public with a very comical attire, including a ridiculous-looking wig.) Pastor also encouraged me with some scriptures and prayer. Then Jeff and I decided that at this time Jeff should return home to be with Judah, who was currently staying up at my parents' house, while another ambulance took me on to Buffalo.

The trip to Buffalo was uneventful. However, when we arrived at ECMC, I felt sorry for the two ambulance crew members because we had to wait in the hallway for quite a while before any hospital attendants came for me. Finally, I was put into a small room where I spent the next several hours thirsty, hungry, confused, and waiting. Many staff members came in to check on me. Because of my concern about having no health insurance, I kept asking if I would be able to go home soon. I was given various answers—some said that I might be able to go home soon; others said that I might have surgery that night; and still others said that I would have to wait seventy-two hours before it could be determined what needed to be done for me since a burn takes that long to fully develop. I desperately wanted water because I had lost a lot of fluid from the burn and had gone a long time without a drink. In addition, I was very hungry since I never did get my supper and was also pregnant. When it was finally decided that I was not having surgery that night, I was greatly relieved to be allowed to drink water and eat a little.

I had arrived at the hospital around 12:00-12:30 A.M. Finally, between 4:30 and 5:30 A.M., I was wheeled to the burn unit where I immediately was whisked into the washroom for debriding (the process of scrubbing off dead, burned skin). This room brought back vivid, horrifying memories. Judah had burned his feet when he was about two, and I remembered the cries of Judah and another burned boy when they were scrubbed. I therefore dreaded what lay ahead of me and also hoped that when Judah came to visit me, he would not find out about this washroom and have any recollection of his past suffering. Thank the Lord, he didn't!

Before the nurses could begin debriding, they had to shave the left side of my head. They apologized for having to do this, but I understood that they needed to have the scalp bare to be able to properly clean the burn. I was, however, surprised that they left the right side long. I figured that they might as well cut all my hair so that at least I would not look awkward with one side of my hair long and one side shaved. (Later I did ask a nurse to cut the right side.) Then the nurses tried to give me an I.V. through which they could administer painkiller for the debriding. But probably because I was so dehydrated from the burn, they had difficulty getting in the I.V. They poked and prodded unsuccessfully in several areas. I had just decided that I would rather endure the full pain of the scrubbing than any more needle pricks when they got in the I.V. To my dread, they informed me that the I.V. would have to be redone later because it was not in well. Putting in an I.V. was well worth the agony, however—I learned to greatly appreciate the I.V. as the means of administering the painkiller before the excruciating pain of the scrapings and scrubbings.

Finally I was taken to my room and told to get as much sleep as possible before 7:00 A.M.—that only gave me about an hour. My fear whenever I tried to rest during that first chaotic night was that I would have nightmares of the accident. I prayed that God would protect not only myself, but also Judah and Amber from such nightmares. Although I kept reliving the terror of the burn during my waking hours, God graciously spared all of us from nightmares about it. I realized as I pondered the accident, that God had also miraculously kept me safe in several other ways. My face and eyes had not been burned, and even though the outside of my left ear had been burned, my hearing was not affected.

When Dr. Seibel saw me for the first time on Friday morning, he instructed the nurses to scrub and dress my wound three times a day. Thankfully, I ended up only being debrided twice daily. He then told me that we would not know if I would need any skin graft until after the seventy-two hours it took for the burn to fully develop. I had assumed that I would spend a few days in the hospital, and then return home and continue my care through outside therapy because Judah's burn had been treated in this way. But my hope of going home soon was looking bleak.

I began to pray that I would not need skin graft surgery because I was very concerned about the cost of the surgery and also assumed that the healing process from the surgery would be more painful and time consuming than just daily therapy of soaking and scrubbing. But God's ways are better than our ways, as I would discover.

While waiting for the final diagnosis of my burn's severity, I actually began to enjoy my stay in the hospital. I learned to daily look for God's blessings. It was fun to meet many new people. The hospital staff let me walk throughout the hospital, so I met not only the staff who helped me, but many others on my frequent walks. I was thrilled to be able to share about my Saviour Jesus Christ with others. I also appreciated the opportunity to get more rest while in the hospital and noticed that the swelling of my varicose vein had decreased. I learned to relax and not worry about how funny I must have looked with my head all wrapped up and tied at the top like a big sack of grain. Although I did not yet know how my looks would be affected from the burn, nor the complete treatment my burn would require, nor how we would pay for all my medical expenses, my faith grew as I learned to cast these worries upon the Lord. I also had to trust God to take care of all my responsibilities at home and elsewhere. I was especially concerned about how Jeff would be able to manage working, home schooling Judah, doing the animal chores, and keeping up with everything else at home. But he handled the extra responsibilities wisely and well.

I also came to appreciate family and friends more. When Jeff and Judah came to visit me on the first day of my hospital stay, I did not know how they would react. I was worried that Jeff would be upset because of my stupidity which caused my accident and resulted in a large financial burden. I also did not know how either Jeff or Judah would react when they saw my ugly bandaged head. But Jeff was very loving and showed no signs of anger or lack of attraction to me, and Judah was not bothered at all by Mom's queer head attire. In fact Judah found my bandaged head quite amusing and joked, "Mom, you look like one of those television cartoon characters whose heads look like the top of a tied bag." (Although he did not know it, he was referring to the Teletubbies.)

God's love was displayed through others more than I had ever remembered experiencing before in my life. Cards and financial gifts poured in. I was pleased with how many people took the time to travel the one and a half hours from my home area to the hospital to visit me. One day I received a very unexpected visit. A man I did not recognize at all entered my room. Since I had just returned from a debridement, I thought that maybe I didn't recognize him because I was not thinking clearly due to the pain medication or to a painfully stinging ointment applied to the burn following the scrubbings or to how miserable I always felt after debriding. But then he explained that he was the father of one of my friends. When she could not come herself to visit me, she had sent her father. I was greatly relieved to know that I **was** thinking clearly and was very impressed that my friend cared enough to send her father to visit me when she couldn't and that he was willing to come on her behalf!

On Monday, April 29, the seventy-two hours for the burn's development were over. The doctor was able to then determine that I did indeed need a skin graft because of the extent of third degree burns. Surgery was set for the following Thursday. I wondered why I had to wait that long and how I could endure the painful scrubbings and boredom of being cooped up in the hospital for that many more days. But God gave daily strength.

In preparation for my surgery, the doctor's first concern was for the safety of the baby. He ordered a sonogram that Monday afternoon to determine if the baby was strong enough to endure the surgery. The sonogram revealed that the baby was fine, but it also showed that the baby was a month further along than the midwives and I had first projected. Now I knew why I had overcome my first trimester sickness sooner than I had expected and why I looked like I was further along than I had thought I was. I, therefore, considered the necessity of this sonogram another unexpected blessing since through it I discovered that I was a month further along than I had been thinking. Additionally, I was informed that if a pregnant mother needs to undergo surgery, the safest time period for the baby to endure surgery is during the second trimester, which was where I was—not a coincidence, I knew!

Jeff came to see me the night before the surgery. The nurse was dressing my wound, and Jeff saw the burn for the first time since the day of the accident. He was amazed to see how ugly the wound was after its full development. He took pictures of it, but said that people might not want to see them. I wanted to have the pictures available to show people how well God can heal, once I was better, and to inform others about how a burn can develop into a more serious wound than its first appearance indicates.

Finally Thursday, May 2, 2002, the day of my surgery arrived. Since I had never had any other surgery before except for a very minor one as an infant, I had no idea what to expect and wondered if I would feel any of the pain. But God gave me peace as I talked to Him about my worries. I came through the surgery fine. The doctor had tried to give me the minimal amount of anesthesia possible to help protect the baby. I actually woke up just as they were wheeling me out of the operation room—I had had just enough medication, praise the Lord! But I still was not sure how the baby had fared. By evening, however,

I knew that the baby was still strong and well because he began kicking me intensively until I ate some crackers. (I had not been able to eat right after the surgery; so by evening, the baby was hungry!) Another blessing, for the sake of the baby, was that I did not require any pain medication after the surgery. I did take some Tylenol for at least one night to help me sleep. It was difficult to sleep because I could only be in one position. The surgeons had taken the skin from my upper left thigh for the graft. Therefore, it hurt to lay on that side. Also, since I had to wear a neck brace to help keep the newly grafted skin in place, I could not turn my head very easily.

Chapter 3

The Recovery

Once the surgery was over, I was able to appreciate the benefits from having surgery. I felt that now I could better sympathize with others who were facing surgery. I also enjoyed relief from the pain of the burn the day immediately following the surgery. Also, I no longer would have to endure the torturous scrubbings. Neither would I have to take time to go to therapy once I got home! So though I had prayed not to need the surgery, I was thankful for it afterwards. An additional blessing was that I did not require skin grafting in any area of my head where my hair grows. Therefore, my hair was eventually able to grow back normally! I was very happy for God's grace once again!

I had to stay in the hospital for five more days after the surgery to make sure that the grafted skin adhered well. One day, after the surgery, I had a pleasant surprise. I was told that there were some relatives in a waiting room who had come to visit me. I could not think of who the relatives would be. I did not expect my elderly parents to travel up to see me. Neither did I think that Melita and my second oldest sister Candy, who also lived with my parents, would come up without them. Since my other sister April lived in New Hampshire, and, as mentioned earlier, my brother Dan lived in Clarks Summit, Pennsylvania, I did not expect them to visit either. When I arrived at the waiting room, I was shocked and thrilled to see April, along with her husband and son. Passing near the hospital on their way to minister at a Christian camp, they stopped to see me. That was a real encouragement!

On Wednesday, May 6, 2002, I finally came home. I was doing well, although it was still hard to walk with my sore left thigh, and I still wore bandages. Right away we enjoyed the kindness of others as our church family, fellow home schoolers, and neighbors brought us food, flowers, and cards.

At my one-month follow-up visit to the hospital, I did need one spot on my head that was not healing well recut. But after that I required no additional doctor care. I did, however, have to wear a tightly-fitted pressure garment to help smooth the grafted skin and to help minimize scarring. (I did not have this garment until about a month after I first came home because it was still being sized.) I decided to wear a hat to improve my appearance while waiting for my hair to grow long enough for both sides to be even and to cover the ugly top part of the pressure garment. I have always despised wearing hats; consequently, wearing a hat daily was very irritable to me. In addition, that summer was very hot, and the garment and hat only increased the sweat and my discomfort. But once again, God helped me to endure these discomforts humbly. I had purposed not to act like I looked any different than anyone else. Therefore, because I drew no unusual attention to myself, people did not treat me as though I looked odd wearing the pressure garment and a hat constantly. My pastor and I joked that the pressure garment made me look like a nun wearing her habit. Some people did tell me after they found out why I was wearing the garment that they had just assumed that I was a nun or something similar.

After I came home from the hospital, I struggled with other physical discomforts. Once again the varicose vein swelled and became extremely painful. But I was able to relieve this problem with the herbal product. At the beginning of June, I developed flu-like symptoms and became weak from not being able to eat enough while pregnant. I remember feeling badly because I was too weak to really enjoy myself and be very pleasant while visiting the Buffalo Zoo with church friends and while attending Jeff's family reunion at his childhood home in Bemus Point, New York (only about fifteen minutes from our house if you take the bridge across Chautauqua Lake). I was very grateful that this condition only lasted for about a week.

There were also other issues to deal with besides physical problems. How to get help to pay for all my burn medical bills was a source of contention for Jeff and me. We finally decided not to accept government help but to pursue avenues of help from people who voluntarily chose to give to us and to also wait on the Lord to provide. We then became excited to see what the Lord would do. We also had to decide what to do about our three goats. I took care of the goats and milked the nanny. I did not know how I would keep up with these chores, take care of a new baby, and fulfill all my other responsibilities. Because I had enjoyed my goats immensely, I wanted to find good homes for them. Never able to find anyone who wanted them, I despondently sold them at an auction.

I finally felt well enough to take a part-time summer job of making pies at a family-run business in Mayville, New York, shortly past the facility where I swam the day of the burn accident. I enjoyed the job very much except that I did get extremely hot wearing the pressure garment (I did not bother to wear the hat while working) and, toward the middle of the summer, my legs and feet began to swell from standing on them so long while pregnant. I had to borrow Amber's shoes, which were one size larger than mine. I began to pray that I would deliver my baby early because my swollen legs were so uncomfortable. The husband of my boss teased me, "One of these days I am going to come in to visit you all while you are making pies and find you lying on the floor, having already delivered the baby." But the baby did not arrive **that** way.

Chapter 4

The Unexpected Delivery

My last day of work was Friday, the thirtieth of August. I then determined to get the baby's room all ready the following week. Although the baby's room, halfway down the short hallway between Jeff's and my bedroom and the kitchen, was very small, seven and a half feet by seven feet, I wanted to make it look as charming as I could for my baby. I intended to paint the walls and ceiling, lay down new carpet, and make my own "Precious Moments" posters to hang on the wall.

This week was also a period of new beginnings for Judah, who would be attending public school after being home schooled through third grade. Jeff and I had decided to send Judah to Chautauqua Lake Central School before we knew that I was pregnant because I had been planning to work full-time, enabling Jeff to study for ministry. Discovering that I was expecting another baby changed Jeff's hopes to attend school, but we still chose to send Judah to public school the following year. Living in the country with no siblings and few neighbors had given Judah little experience in developing proper social skills. Although he had regularly associated with other children through church and home school activities, Judah was naturally introverted, and thus Jeff and I hoped that exposure to more children would strengthen Judah's social skills. I fretted over Judah's dread of attending school. Fortunately, working on the baby's room helped distract me from worrying about Judah during his first week of school. Although attending public school was the most painful period of adjustment during Judah's childhood, he did learn to socialize better with others and to enjoy the blessings of new friendships.

With the help of two friends from church, I was able to complete most of the baby's room by the end of that week. Jeff laid the carpet on Saturday morning. Then I began to pull the baby items out of storage to arrange in the baby room. Prior to this year I had stored most of my extra items either at my parents' house or in a large shed halfway between their house and our trailer since our trailer was so small, fifty-five feet by ten feet. Once the babies started coming, I realized how blessed I was to be married to a talented carpenter. When Judah was due, Jeff had built an addition onto the front of our bedroom and part of the hallway as a bedroom/laundry room. With a second baby on the way, Jeff built a small two-story addition onto the other end of the trailer in front of the living room. We called this addition "the tower" since it stood fairly high above the flat roofed, one-story trailer. We used the tower mostly for storage, and I had moved most of the baby items from my parents' house and the shed to the top floor of the tower once Jeff had finished it.

Although it was challenging for me being nine months pregnant to move the baby items down the ladder from the second floor, I was eager to get the room all ready for the baby. I faced some other complications while trying to move the baby items. I had to take apart the changing table in order to fit it through the narrow bedroom doorway. Then I noticed that the crib needed some touch-up painting before I could set it up. I asked Jeff to paint the crib. Busy working on a new deck in front of the tower, Jeff took the crib to the barn to paint later. When I noticed the car seat in storage, I debated whether I should get it out to wash and put into the car right then or wait until later since I was not due for a few more weeks. I decided to get the car seat ready right then.

Late in the afternoon, while carrying baby clothes down the ladder, I noticed that I was leaking water. I sent someone out to tell Jeff that apparently my water had just broken. Jeff, intent on the building project, barely paid any attention. Soon I began light labor. I had not expected to go into labor so early since Judah had been nearly two weeks late. The early labor should not have surprised me since I had prayed for an early delivery. As the labor progressed, I was very thankful that I **had** decided to pull out the car seat from storage and clean it and that I had persevered to finish most of the baby room that week. I also reflected on the surprise shower the ladies of the church had given me just two days ago. I do not believe that it was coincidence for all these events to have happened that week. God's timetable is always right on schedule!

However, Jeff and I did not rush to do much about the baby immediately since we were remembering my thirty-two-hour-long labor with Judah. So Jeff continued working on the deck, and I kept doing light work around the home. There was one item with which I did need to deal right away, however. I had to make plans for a midwife. Ironically, my regular midwife was away that weekend. When Gladys told me, "Don't have the baby between September 4 and 8 because I will be gone then," I had laughed, thinking that there was no reason to worry about an early delivery since I had been so late delivering

Judah. Wisely, Gladys had given me the names of a few other midwives. Gladys also had the foresight to provide Jeff with advice in case the baby arrived before we reached her residence in Pennsylvania since we live an hour away. (Rather than traveling to her patients' houses, Gladys required expectant mothers to come to a clinic in her home for delivery.) After several attempts, I finally reached Jenny, one of the midwives that Gladys had suggested. Since my labor was still light, Jenny told me just to keep in touch with her.

Around 9:00 P.M. my labor pain became too severe for me to continue any work. Around midnight, Jeff called Jenny again. She told him how to check my progress. Since I was only slightly dilated at the time, Jeff remained on the couch with me, timing my contractions. Jeff was sure that we had a long wait ahead of us based upon my long labor with Judah. I was no longer so certain of this. My labor with Judah had been prolonged by an unusual circumstance—his head had become stuck on my bladder. My water had not broken before labor with Judah either. Jeff tired of timing my contractions, but I could tell that they were becoming more intense, more often, and lasting longer. Around 2:30 A.M. I insisted that he check me again. He hesitated, but when he did, he felt the baby's head. He called Jenny immediately, and she said, "come!" The plan was that we were to both meet at Gladys' house since we both knew where that was. Jenny had about a forty-five-minute drive, and we had an hour drive.

We woke up Judah and loaded into the car. Jeff had prepared the green Taurus station wagon well, putting down the back seat to make a "bed" of boards and cushions for me. I did not realize until after I had returned home and opened my bathroom cupboard that he had also taken all the towels stored there. I did not tell Jeff, but I knew when we left home that I would not make it to the midwife's; and due to my agony, I did not want to wait another whole hour anyway!

Five miles from home, as we came to the four-corners in the small village of Panama, New York, I heard Judah say, "Oh no! We can't get through!" I panicked! Caution tape was spread around the four-corners. When Jeff could see no reason for caution, he assumed that it was only a prank, reached through his window, tore down the tape, and drove on. That was a relief! Five minutes later, I told Jeff to pull over because I felt the urge to push. He pulled over, took a quick glance, said that I was not ready, and drove on. I thought that he should have waited. In about five more minutes, once again I insisted that he pull over. He did, but also got the car stuck in the deep ditch. As he tried to get the car out of the ditch, I yelled, "Forget the car! I have to push now!" He got out and found the baby's head already visible. With one foot on the road and one in the ditch, Daddy prepared to deliver baby. A passing fireman stopped to see if we needed help. Jeff shouted, "Yes, my wife is having a baby, and the car is stuck in the ditch!" When the fireman started to dial 9-1-1, Jeff told him that we did not need 9-1-1 because the baby was almost out. We did, however, need help getting the car out of the ditch. The fireman then drove off to try to find help at such an unreasonable hour.

During all this commotion, poor Judah did not know what to do. He got out of the car once, but immediately got back in, not wanting to see the actual birth. Jeff continued to coach me. With one or two pushes, the baby's head was out, and Jeff said, "Your baby wants to see you." He then told me to push again. Soon the baby was out! Jeff yelled, "It's a boy!" I was greatly relieved, but Jeff had a brief moment of panic. When he saw the baby's greenish color, *stillborn* entered his mind. Then the baby began crying. He was okay! Jeff chose not to cut the cord since Gladys had told us that it was beneficial to leave the cord attached for fifteen to thirty minutes because it continues supplying the baby with nutritious blood. Jeff, therefore, just wrapped the baby in a towel and laid him on my stomach.

Jubal Asher Samuelson was born September 8, 2002, on the side of the road just outside of Clymer, New York, about twenty-five minutes from our home. Once again God had answered several specific prayers that I had prayed concerning the birth. I had prayed that he would be born without my needing any hospitalization since I already had such a large medical bill from the burn. I had prayed that the baby would not come during the times that I normally was tutoring or babysitting. I had also prayed that the baby would come at a time when Judah could be present (thus not during school). Since Jubal was born around 3:50 on Sunday morning, all these requests were answered. I also was extremely grateful that my labor with Jubal was much shorter than with Judah!

Jubal's name is significant. Jubal is a male form of Jubilee. If he had been a girl, he would have been named Jubilee. Jubilee is the name of an important Jewish celebration. In the year of Jubilee, those in bondage were set free. Jubal was my celebration after nine years of waiting for another child. His name also reminded me of the freedom from sin that Jesus Christ makes possible to all who believe in Him. Asher was my father's middle name, and it means happiness. Such celebrations as the Year of Jubilee and the birth of a baby are certainly times of great happiness!

After Jubal's safe delivery, Jeff got back into the car and began to rock it back and forth to get it out of the ditch. This was extremely uncomfortable for my stomach, but he finally got the car out. Then we had to decide, "Do we wait for the fireman to return, or do we go on to the midwife?" Although we hated to leave the fireman in a lurch, we decided that it was best to go on to have baby and mom checked and to get baby into a warmer environment.

We all were filled with mixed emotions. Jeff was a very proud father having delivered his own son. Judah was happy to receive the baby **brother** for which he had prayed. Mom was relieved to be done with labor! I also was proud that I had been able to deliver the baby on my own with Jeff's help. Actually, throughout the pregnancy, I had secretly wished for Jeff to deliver the baby, although I had not planned it to be along the roadside. I began to both cry and laugh with joy. Now that I could talk again, I talked nonstop. I had so much for which to praise the Lord!

Our adventurous trip to the midwife was not quite over. Suddenly the window beside Jubal and me began to roll down on its own. It continued to do this even though Jeff kept rolling it back up. Finally, Jeff got out to see what the problem was. Praise God, it was something silly and minor—a box containing a flashlight had fallen onto the window-control knob. Jeff removed the box, and we continued the rest of the trip uneventfully.

When we finally arrived at Gladys' home, Jenny and Gladys' nurse, Monica, came rushing out. They assumed that we must have already had the baby since it had taken us so long to get there. Jenny then cut the cord and removed my placenta before I got out of the car. Mom and baby were fine, but Jubal was cold and hungry. We got Jubal dressed, and Mom fed him. We all had a good time discussing Jubal's birth and enjoying some light refreshments. We had arrived at the midwife's around 4:30 A.M. and left to go home around 7:30. I wanted to get home so that Judah could rest more, and the baby could have a more comfortable place to sleep. Jeff and I needed rest too. I also wanted to see my family before they went to church so that they would know that we were all fine, and they could see the baby. The trip home was much calmer than the trip going. I was excited to see the actual birth spot of Jubal in daylight and without being consumed with the pain of giving birth.

Chapter 5

The Blessings Abound

When we got home, Jeff immediately headed to the barn to paint the crib that he had not had time to paint before the baby's early arrival. Judah and I scurried next door with Jubal to show him off to all my family who still lived in the farmhouse and to tell them about his unusual birth. My parents; two oldest sisters, Melita and Candy; Amber; and her older brother, Justin, were all excited to see Jubal and hear the story of his birth. While they were admiring him, Justin ran outside to get the newspaper. When he brought in the *Post Journal*, he showed us the front page. It featured a large picture of Jeff, Judah, and me with an article about my burn. A friend of mine, Shelly, had arranged to have the article written, hoping that it would help bring in some financial aid for my medical bills, which it did. I was pleased with the article and that it included the credit we had given to the Lord during our interview for all God's care throughout the burn tragedy and since. I was amused to read in the article that my baby was due in a few weeks, and there I was holding him!

After my family left for church, Jeff, Judah, Jubal, and I all had a chance to rest. I did some projects around the house first, however, and thought *Wow! I just had a baby!* I didn't even feel like it. It just felt great to be able to move freely and normally again!

That afternoon Judah went to a church picnic. He came home complaining, "I don't want to be asked another question about how the baby was born!" But I, still in a world of disbelief that I actually had a baby again, loved to look at him and kept praising God for him. I was especially amused with his feet. They were very long and skinny since he was a long baby (twenty-two inches) but not yet filled out, having arrived a few weeks early (weighed seven pounds).

Following Jubal's birth, God continued to shower us with His gracious blessings. The newspaper article resulted in a flow of letters, cards, and monetary gifts even from people we did not know. I also was thrilled whenever people told me that the article had encouraged them and truly glorified God.

The news reporter who wrote the first article wanted to write another one about Jubal's birth. So two weeks after the first article, a second one appeared on the front page of our local paper displaying a picture of Jeff, Judah, baby Jubal, and myself sitting in the back of Jubal's birthing bed—the Taurus—with its back hatch opened (see picture). Praise God, more cards, notes, and financial gifts were sent following the second article! When people saw Jubal and me after both articles were featured in the paper (it was easy for them to recognize me even if they did not know me because of my pressure garment), they commented on how much they had enjoyed the articles and how amazing Jubal's birth was. Again, in response to their comments, I had more opportunities to give God the glory.

The article about Jubal's birth also accomplished something else. Apparently, when the fireman who had gone to get help for us while the car was stuck during Jubal's birth returned and found us gone, the helpers were hesitant to believe him. When we heard this report, we were amused, but also felt badly for the fireman. Although I did not know the name of the fireman at that time, I knew his fire station and was able to contact that station, informing them that his bizarre story about a couple with their car stuck in the ditch while the wife was delivering a baby around 3:45 A.M. **was** true. The newspaper article also confirmed his story.

Material aid kept pouring in! Individual friends gave us various needed baby items. Several groups also helped us. Compeer, a group for which I am a volunteer, held a benefit spaghetti dinner for us. A local Christian band gave a concert to help raise money for us. Judah's fourth grade class held a baked goods sale to help. Our church gave us money. Salvation Army and Creche, a group that helps needy children, also gave us gifts.

December 4, 2002, was my last trip to Buffalo for a checkup on my burn. All looked good. I hoped that the doctor would tell me that I would not have to wear my pressure garment any more, but he wanted me to continue wearing it until April 2003, fulfilling about a year. Oh well, God had enabled me to endure wearing the garment thus far, and He would provide me the grace to continue wearing it as long as necessary. (I actually did discontinue wearing it before April when I recognized that I had healed well enough and would make no more progress wearing it any longer).

The year of 2002 was nearly over. God had brought me through the most physically challenging year of my life. He had taught me to depend upon Him for everything and for each moment. He had humbled me, but also showed me amazing love and grace. He had saved me from fire for the second time in my life. First, He had saved me from the eternal fires of hell when I asked Him to forgive me of my sin. Secondly, He rescued me from the fire of my stove. Wow! I truly have a lot for which to thank my Lord and Saviour!

    I knew that there would be many more challenges ahead of me, such as dealing with my large medical bills. (At the time, I had no idea of the important lessons God had prepared to teach me through major challenges a few years later.) As I had already seen God's miraculous provisions, I looked forward to discovering how He would continue to meet our needs and bless us, even through pain.

Praise be to God, as of 2010, all my medical bills have been paid except for the one main bill from the hospital; and the hospital has graciously agreed to allow us to pay a small amount on that bill each month.

Notes

1. The "bride of Christ" is the "body" or "Church" of Christ. This body is not a physical body, nor is the "Church" a building. Rather these are terms used to collectively refer to all people who have chosen to follow Christ as their Saviour. In heaven, all such believers are considered to be the bride of Christ.
2. Revelation 20:15 says, "And anyone not found written in the Book of Life was cast into the lake of fire." Believe me, from my brief experience with fire, no one wants to spend eternity in a lake of fire! But how can you be saved from this eternal damnation? Luke 13:3 and 5 says, ". . . unless you repent you will all likewise perish." The Bible is clear that we all need to repent because Romans 3:23 says, "for all have sinned and fall short of the glory of God." The Bible also says, "the wages of sin is death," Romans 6:23. The lake of fire is called "the second death," Revelation 20:14. Therefore unless we repent we face the wage or punishment for sin of eternity in the lake of fire. But praise God for the second part of Romans 6:23! It goes on to say, "but the gift of God is eternal life in Christ Jesus our Lord." Jesus took the punishment we deserved by dying on the cross for us. Repent of your sin, and "Believe on the Lord Jesus Christ, and you will be saved," Acts 16:31. Then you can enjoy that gift of eternal life in heaven with God rather than suffer eternal punishment in the lake of fire. Please feel free to contact me at Lydia Samuelson P.O. Box 67, Ashville, New York 14710, or at jcsam1@windstream.net, if you have any questions.

Epilogue

Because so many people gave very generously and graciously to us after my accident, I wanted to be able to do something to show my gratitude. Knowing that I did not have extra money to give, I wondered what I could do. As mentioned in the forward, I decided that one way I could thank others was by writing this story and mentioning in it ways that people gave. Shortly after my accident I heard about another way that I could give that would not require money. But I had to wait for the right opportunity. Part two of this book shares the story of the second way that I gave.

Sacrifice's Challenges

Part Two

To Ryan whose suffering and perseverance through his suffering encouraged me to never give up.

Chapter 1

The Right Opportunity

So you have decided to make a special sacrifice for the Lord and others. Are you sure that you are up to the challenge? Oh I don't mean simply the challenge of the pain and suffering of the sacrifice itself, but also of numerous obstacles that will be sure to stand in your way as you make preparations for the sacrifice. You may often get very discouraged, wondering if God even wants you to make this sacrifice. You may become angry, questioning why God would not send His blessings upon you, His servant, who has so willingly offered yourself to Him for this great sacrifice. Don't be discouraged, my friend, I discovered that if God does want you to make the sacrifice, He will enable you to overcome each obstacle.

As mentioned in "Pain's Blessings," I was looking for a way to show my appreciation for how much others had given me after my burn accident. Knowing that I had neither extra money nor any special talent, I was unsure of what I could do. But during 2002 I heard about two individuals with the same need. Around the time of my burn accident, our family learned that my nephew, Ryan Samuelson, born October 23, 2001, had autosomal recessive polycistic kidney disease (ARPKD). This rare genetic disease gradually destroys the kidney with cysts. Cysts also form on the liver, leading to fibrosis (crumbling) of the liver. Shocked and saddened, we discovered that eventually Ryan would need another kidney and liver. In the fall of 2002, I also learned that Phil Sweeney, a deacon of our church, needed a kidney transplant. I was willing to offer a kidney to either Ryan or Phil. But when told that Ryan would probably need a cadaver kidney from another child, I did not, at that time, seriously pursue donating to him. I attended an informative meeting held at

Panama Baptist Church for members considering donating to Phil. But since I was close to my due date for Jubal, I was not a good candidate for Phil either. (Our Pastor's wife, Lisabeth Colton, graciously gave one of her kidneys to Phil on March 5, 2003. The kidney lasted for about a year. Sadly, after the kidney failed, Phil gradually weakened and went home to be with his Saviour on September 16, 2005.)

A little over a year after Jubal's birth, I learned of a friend who needed a kidney transplant. His kidneys had been damaged by medicine and then severely aggravated due to a serious car accident. When I saw my friend, Jeff Alonge, in the store one day, I asked him if he had any possible kidney donors yet. He told me "no." I began the process of having my kidney tested to see if it would be a match for him. I passed all the tests, and a date was set for the transplant surgery in June 2004. The day before the surgery I received a call from Robin, my transplant coordinator, telling me of a problem. While reviewing the pictures of my right kidney (the one to be used for the transplant) in preparation for the surgery, the doctor noticed that the kidney was smaller than a normal adult's kidney. Since Jeff was significantly bigger than I, my undersized kidney would probably not have been sufficient to sustain him. Although he and I were very disappointed, we recognized that my kidney would not be the most efficient kidney for Jeff. A few months later, on November 23, 2004, God blessed Jeff Alonge with a cadaver kidney that has adequately meant his need.

In the meantime, I struggled with understanding why God would allow me to pass all the tests to be a kidney donor for Jeff Alonge, only to stop the procedure the day before the scheduled surgery. I had, however, prayed that God would close the door if I should not donate the kidney to Jeff, and He did. Although God had given me a desire to help another by being a living organ donor, He was challenging my willingness to accept and await **His** timing for such a sacrifice.

Jeff's transplant doctor did tell me that my kidney would be a good candidate for a child. Since Ryan had not yet received a kidney, I told his mom that if the doctors decided to consider a living donor rather than a cadaver, my small kidney might work well for him. But it was finally decided to use his father's kidney since he was so closely related; thus, hopefully his kidney would be less of a risk for rejection by Ryan's body. The kidney transplant took place on October 26, 2005, when Ryan was only four years old. Ryan's body did not reject the kidney, and after a long recovery, Ryan finally was able to enjoy somewhat more of a normal childhood life for a few years. I rejoiced that at last Ryan and Jubal, a year younger than Ryan, were able to play together.

For the time being, I set aside my desire to help another as a living donor. Perhaps God did not want me to make that kind of sacrifice. In the meantime many changes took place in the Samuelson household, especially in 2006. In

February of that year, we started our own home church. The following October, we moved from the trailer to the farmhouse. Melita had moved to another house a little less than a quarter mile down the road with my mother (my father had gone home to be with Jesus November 13, 2004). Amber had moved in with a friend, and Justin was attending college in Ohio. Candy was the only one of my family to stay in the farmhouse. The approximately one hundred sixty-year-old farmhouse was in need of much repair and remodeling to fit my family's needs. One of the first projects that Jeff did was to make a cozy bedroom for Candy in the back of the house. She shares the kitchen, living room, and two bathrooms, all on the first floor, as well as the laundry area in the basement with us. Jeff was able to remodel the bedrooms for all of us before we moved in. Since moving in, he has added two bathrooms for a total of three and remodeled the living room. He plans to do more work as the Lord provides the time and money. In the meantime, we are very grateful for a big house with three bathrooms and the rooms that Jeff has so attractively redone.

Moving into a much larger home in October 2006, was a real blessing because on November 14, 2006, I had our third son, Joram David Samuelson. This time Jeff did not have to deliver the baby himself. I had two very wise and experienced midwives who came to our home to deliver the baby. It was truly a blessing that the midwives were able to aid me at our home since Jeff was injured at the time and limited in his physical activities. Candy fell in love with the baby at once and has become a second "mother" to him. As a toddler, he called her "I yah." Candy has been a big asset to me around the house, helping care for Joram and aiding with household chores. In turn we help her by providing her with much of her transportation needs since she cannot drive, and we are instrumental in guiding her with decisions and activities that are difficult for her as an adult with less-than-average mental capacity.

In the fall of 2008, after we had had time to adjust to the many changes of moving, having a third child, starting a church, and having my sister live with us, my thoughts once again turned toward the possibility of helping Ryan, who had turned seven that October. His liver was deteriorating enough to begin serious search for a liver donor. Ryan was on a cadaver transplant list, but was still rather low on the list— one higher on the list is more likely to receive an available cadaver liver. Peter, Ryan's father, was the first living donor candidate. Hopefully, if Pete could donate the liver as he had already donated a kidney, Ryan's body would be less likely to reject either organ coming from the same source. Early in 2009, Pete went for blood work to see if he would indeed be a good match as a liver donor for Ryan. Oddly enough, he was not.

I remember the day that Ryan's mother Dawn called me to ask if I was still willing to be a possible donor for Ryan. She was very upset that Pete had failed and also expressed guilt to even approach me as a possible donor since I was the mother of two young children. (At the time, Jubal was six years old, and Joram was two.) I told her that after discussing it with Jeff, I would get back in touch with her. Both Jeff and I felt that we should be willing to help our relatives and would pray for God to close the door if I was not to be the donor. As long as He kept the door open, we would pursue the donor process.

Dawn had told me that Jeff's younger brother Dave would be tested first since he was a blood relative. Oddly, once again, Dave's blood work revealed that he was not a good match for Ryan. I was to be tested next.

Perhaps the day I went for blood work should have been a cue to me of how the whole testing process was going to be—full of challenges. Thankfully, I was able to do the blood work in New York and just ship it by UPS to Pittsburgh. In February 2009, I went to Jamestown, the closest city at about ten miles from our home, for my blood work. However, when I reached the office on Prather Avenue where I had been taking Candy for her annual blood work, it appeared unusually quiet. Upon entering the main lobby, I read the sign posted outside the office door, "moved to . . ." Fortunately, I only had to travel less than half a mile further to the new location on Foote Avenue. At the phlebotomy office desk, the nurse told me that, although as a living donor I did not have to pay for the blood work, I would need to pay a ten dollar drawing fee. Knowing that the blood testing fee would be covered, I was totally unprepared to pay anything. I had no money with me and was told that I could not use a credit card to pay. The nurse graciously let me get my blood work done first and then go get the money.

Being able to take the blood work with me when I went to pick up the money was very convenient because there was a plaza only about a mile down the road that had both a UPS store and a Quality Markets—I could mail the blood work and get the ten dollars in one stop. At the plaza, I first went into an office that I thought was the UPS store. When I asked the worker for guidance to properly prepare the package for mailing the blood work, she politely informed me that I needed to go to the UPS store at the opposite end of the plaza. Woops! Not realizing that there was also a USPS in the plaza, I had just assumed I was entering the UPS store when I saw the "USP" letters. Rather embarrassed, I left the United States Post Office! I then went on to Quality, which was closer to the post office than was the UPS office. After getting the needed ten dollars at Quality, I found the correct UPS store. I put my blood work into a UPS envelope, but then was confused about the correct mailing address to use. The address on the shipping label included in the blood work packet was different from the address listed on the blood work directions sheet. I called Pittsburgh and thankfully was able to reach my transplant coordinator right away (normally she is hard to reach). Mimi, my coordinator, confirmed that she would safely receive the blood work if it were sent to the address on the shipping label. I scooted out of the store, relieved to finally get the blood work mailed, only to look down and, to my dismay, stare at the blood work direction sheet still in my hand. I had used the paper to call Pittsburgh for the correct address and forgot to then slip it into the envelope. Without it, how would Pittsburgh know whose blood was in those vials?! Once again, feeling like a total fool, I rushed back to the UPS store and explained my dilemma to the worker. We finally decided that we would have to cautiously cut a small slit in the envelope, slip in the paperwork, and then carefully tape the slit. At last the blood work was ready to go, and I could return to the phlebotomist with the ten dollars.

A few weeks later Pittsburgh called to inform me that my blood work matched Ryan's very well—how ironic that I, the non-blood relative, tested as a positive match for Ryan. April 6 to 9 was set as the date for me to go to Pittsburgh for further testing.

Chapter 2

Waiting and Wondering

My sister-in-law Dawn told me that possibly, if all my tests cleared positive for me to be Ryan's donor, the transplant could be the week following the testing. I, therefore, tried to make as many plans as I could just in case if the surgery was set that soon. Since I live in the country with few nearby neighbors available to help, my home school friend Liz arranged extra help for me during the daytime while Jeff and Candy were at work and Judah was at school. Liz contacted other home school families via e-mail asking for students to volunteer for one day to help me. I asked neighbors (in my area, neighbors may include friends who live two to three miles away) to sit with Mom for an hour a day to relieve Melita. Normally Candy would stay with Mom for about an hour a day to give Melita a chance to get out of the house, but I did not know if I could spare Candy after my surgery. I also arranged for some meals to be brought in from Panama Baptist Church, where we used to attend and where Candy still attends, while I was away for the testing and then as needed if I did become Ryan's donor.

I wanted to do a special event with Jubal and Joram before the testing, not knowing when I might be able to do anything fun with them again if I were to be the donor. The week before the scheduled testing the circus came to the ice arena in Jamestown. I wanted to take the kids to the circus since they had never been to one before. Unexpectedly, a health issue arose with Candy. I would have to take her to an early doctor appointment the morning after the circus. Therefore, I would have preferred to attend the afternoon show to avoid a late bedtime since I had to get the children and me ready to leave fairly early the next morning for Candy's appointment. Unfortunately, my friend with whom I was planning to attend the circus could not get out of work early enough for the afternoon show. I asked myself, *Should I add stress to my already hectic week preparing to go to Pittsburgh by going to the circus, especially in the evening?* Finally I did decide to go. Jubal thoroughly enjoyed it, but it was long and very late for Joram. Since Joram really likes elephants, I decided to wait for them and then leave right after the elephants' performance. Ironically, the elephants were the **last** event of the evening! Although it was a school night, the show did not finish until 10 P.M. Part of me regretted that I took time to go to the circus because I did get sick within a few days. However, hearing Jubal enthusiastically tell Dad, "You should have seen the . . . at the circus," gratified me.

The morning after the circus I took Candy to her appointment with her primary physician. She then ordered an ultrasound for Candy. Since the doctor felt that it was urgent to have the ultrasound as soon as possible, and I had no guarantee of my schedule after the following week of testing, we set the ultrasound appointment for the next day, Thursday.

Jeff had been sick that week, and as mentioned earlier, I, being stressed and worn out, easily caught his illness. It appeared to be a flu/cold combination. Jeff and I usually have the flu for only about a day. But no matter how many herbal and natural remedies we tried, we hung onto this sickness for several days. I was especially concerned because I did not know if Pittsburgh would let me be tested if I was ill. Since we did not have a very reliable vehicle and Dawn knew exactly where to go in Pittsburgh, I was planning to ride down with her and her two children, Ryan and his older sister Taylor, age nine. We were going to leave for Pittsburgh on Monday afternoon. Still not feeling very well on Sunday and not wanting to pass on any sickness to Ryan, I called Dawn to let her know my about my concern of exposing Ryan to my illness and about whether or not I could still be tested, not being completely well yet. Knowing how long Pete, Dawn, and Ryan had been waiting for him to get a liver, I fretted about causing them any more delay if the testing had to be rescheduled due to my sickness. To my relief, Dawn responded very positively. She said not to worry about Ryan. She herself was concerned about another issue with Ryan—the left side of his face appeared droopy that day, perhaps showing some paralysis. Therefore, Dawn was anxious to take Ryan to Pittsburgh anyway to be examined. We agreed to get in touch again in the morning once I found out if I would still be able to be tested even though I still was not completely well.

I wondered, *Is God using this illness to shut the door to my being Ryan's liver donor? Is Satan trying to discourage me from making this sacrifice for Ryan? Or is God testing my faith and sincerity to sacrifice?*

I called Pittsburgh early Monday morning. Not reaching Mimi, I left a message. I tried a few more time to reach Mimi with no success. Although

I still had some lingering cold-like symptoms and was weak from losing weight, I was thankful to be feeling much better. By 1:00 P.M. Jeff told me that, although I had not yet heard from Mimi, I should just plan to go since I needed to leave that afternoon, and I had a lot to prepare at home for while I was gone and still needed to pack. Finally, at 3:00 P.M., Mimi called and said, "As long as you feel well enough to come, then come." I was relieved to receive this confirmation before Dawn, along with Ryan and Taylor, picked me up around 4:00 P.M.

On Tuesday I had all the physical tests done to see if I was healthy enough to be a donor and if I was truly compatible for Ryan. Wednesday morning I met with various members of the transplant team, such as a social worker, an anesthesiologist, and Dr. Humar, the surgeon. Things went fairly smoothly until partway through my meeting with Dr. Humar. Since my appointments had been scheduled with some free time between them, I had intended to meet Dawn and her children for breakfast sometime between the morning appointments. But the appointments lasted longer than I anticipated, and I got no break. I was very hungry since I had lost weight while sick and had not been able to eat until late afternoon the day before due to required fasting for some of the tests. While standing with Dr. Humar, observing his diagram of the liver, I suddenly felt light-headed and woozy. I told Dr. Humar, "I think I need to sit down." I explained that I was recovering from sickness and was now feeling very hungry but had not eaten breakfast yet. I had had some coffee, but it had only intensified the sudden low drop in my blood sugar. Dr. Humar asked Mimi to bring me some juice, which revived me, and our meeting continued, but I worried that this little mishap might discourage the transplant team from considering me strong enough to be a donor.

I was encouraged, however, when the doctor told me that based upon the earlier tests, I did not need to have the liver biopsy, which had been temporarily scheduled for Thursday. I hoped, therefore, to be able to go home the next morning. I had, however, enjoyed the week with Dawn and her children. My family is rarely able to take vacations; therefore, it had seemed like a mini-vacation to me, not having to worry about the daily home chores. I had also enjoyed the extra blessing of being introduced to Panara Bread, the restaurant connected to the hotel where we stayed. Since I make my own bread from home-ground flour, I was thrilled to discover a place away from home that had delicious, wholesome, homemade bread and other healthy, organic products.

Rarely being separated from my children, I was eager to get home to my family. The unusual and challenging events of Thursday prolonged the time before I could see my family. Dawn, still concerned about Ryan's left side of the face, took him to Children's Hospital of Pittsburgh (where he had had his kidney transplant and would have his liver transplant) for blood work and a checkup. Unsure of what was happening with him, the hospital admitted

Ryan. Dawn, now unable to leave Ryan to take Taylor and me home, called her husband Pete to drive down to get us. My heart sank—it was at least a three-hour trip from their home in Bemus Point, New York. I would not be able to get home as soon as I had hoped. Even if Pete could leave right away and drive directly to Pittsburgh without any problems, he was going to have trouble getting through Pittsburgh that day because a memorial service was being held there for three policemen who had been killed the previous weekend during a domestic dispute. Policemen from all over the United States and even from some foreign countries had come to Pittsburgh for the service. The street directly in front of the hospital and the next parallel street below it were lined with parked police cars. Pete would have to park some distance away from the hospital and walk to it. Then we did not know when we would be able to get back out of the city. While waiting for Pete to arrive, Taylor and I entertained ourselves walking along the streets looking at the police cars and trying to find ones from our own area. Taylor also enjoyed taking pictures of police cars parked bumper to bumper.

Dawn and I had another complication. Both of our cell phones' batteries were low. Furthermore, I had forgotten my charger at home, and she could not find hers. Praise the Lord, the batteries lasted long enough for Dawn and me to communicate with one another while she stayed with Ryan in the hospital and Taylor and I ran errands or just walked around until Pete arrived. Pete was actually talking to me while he was walking through the hospital trying to locate us when my phone finally died! While waiting for the city to clear of the visiting policemen, we watched live broadcasts of the memorial service. Then when each hearse finally left the service, we observed it actually pass directly by the hospital (the memorial service took place at the Peterson Event Center of the University of Pittsburgh, located just above the hospital).

Throughout this frustrating day of waiting, wondering, and wandering, I had spent some time with Ryan. I wanted to cry as I observed his pain and agony. Ryan was hungry and thirsty because he had not been allowed to eat or drink since the doctors intended to perform some procedures that required fasting from food and water. After seeing some of Ryan's suffering firsthand and recognizing that he has endured major suffering most of his life, I resolved more than ever to pursue donating part of my liver to him. I was also impressed with this seven year old's determination to persevere through suffering and with his general good nature in spite of his persistent agony.

That memorable Thursday I came to appreciate the strength Dawn needed to remain faithfully beside her son while watching him suffer intensely. As I enjoyed time with Taylor, I discovered what a mature nine year old she was. She had learned to be a real encouragement to Ryan, and a great asset to her parents, helping with Ryan. She had also developed a very independent, uncomplaining attitude while her parents were preoccupied with Ryan's needs.

At last around six o'clock that Thursday evening, Pittsburgh was clear enough for Pete, Taylor, and me to head home. The doctors did not yet know what to do for Ryan, and while my heart ached to leave him and Dawn behind at the hospital, I was excited to finally be going home!

Although many specialists examined Ryan, no conclusion was ever made to explain why Ryan's left facial side had temporarily appeared droopy. However, as we would soon discover once his liver was removed, the liver was in such poor condition that it must have been causing many complications in Ryan's poor sick body. In fact, Ryan was in and out of the children's hospital in Pittsburgh frequently the month prior to his liver transplant.

Although quite confident that I had passed all the physical requirements to be Ryan's liver donor, I was concerned that two other factors could cause the transplant team to question my eligibility as donor—the episode of my blood sugar dropping and my acknowledgement to the social worker about my eating struggles (often not eating enough and then, when I become ravenous, eating too much too fast). I was right. The Wednesday after the testing Mimi called. She told me that all the tests looked good, but that there were two concerns of the transplant team. One concern was that I would not eat enough and would do too much too soon for my liver to grow back well. The second concern was that, without any health insurance, I would be personally responsible for the costs if I did develop any health problems from not eating adequately. The team decided to have me come back to Pittsburgh for an evaluation at an eating disorder clinic. I did not want to do this, but was willing to for Ryan's sake. I asked if I could simply meet with someone from my own area for an evaluation. But Mimi said, "No, I'm sorry, but the team really wants you to be evaluated here." (There was an eating disorder clinic connected with the University of Pittsburgh Medical Center {UPMC}, and Montefiore, the hospital where I had had my tests and would have the transplant surgery, was also part of UPMC.) Mimi said that I needed to schedule the appointment myself, but she would call me back to let me know whom to call to schedule it. She also reassured me that I would not have to pay for this evaluation. Two days later, Friday, Mimi called back with the contact information I needed.

I was unable to reach anyone to schedule the appointment for several days. I was becoming frustrated and impatient and felt badly that my personal problem meant more uncertain waiting for Ryan and his parents. At last, the following Wednesday, I reached the right person to make my appointment. It was set for the following Thursday, April 30.

On Tuesday, April 28, two days before my appointment in Pittsburgh, the eating disorder clinic called to inform me that **I** would have to pay for the evaluation. I was shocked and worried. I knew that I did not have the money to pay for it, and Mimi had told me that the cost would be covered. I tried to reach Mimi right away, but could not. There was nothing I could do but pray.

Once again I wondered if God was closing the door for me to be Ryan's donor. But finally, late Wednesday afternoon, the day before my appointment, Mimi called. "You do **not** have to pay for the evaluation," she told me. *Okay, God, the door is still open. I will continue this pursuit for Ryan.*

My father- and mother-in-law, Phil and Sondra Samuelson, drove Jubal, Joram, and me to Pittsburgh for my appointment. Grandma and Grandpa took the boys to lunch and to a massive flower show while I went to my appointment. While waiting at the clinic for my appointment, I felt extremely embarrassed. *Why am I here?* I thought. *I know I'll eat enough to recover. I just don't eat regularly like I should. Sometimes I don't eat enough, but then I make up for that by eating too much. Yeah, that's why I'm here,* I admitted to myself. I have developed some unusual, uncontrolled eating habits, even though I pride myself on usually eating "healthy" foods. And even when I think I eat a lot, I may not get sufficient protein for the liver to rejuvenate. (I rarely eat meat and don't always eat much from other protein sources either.) I had to honestly confess that I had caused my own inconvenient shame requiring an eating disorder evaluation.

Finally, Cathy, my evaluator was ready to see me. She was very kind, which helped me feel less nervous. I have always been concerned about the times that I eat too much, admitting that overeating is wrong and being very ashamed and embarrassed about it. Cathy expressed a different concern. "I'm not worried about when you eat too much," she told me after requesting me to list how much and what I might eat for an average day. "I'm worried that you don't eat enough."

I left the evaluation feeling uncertain and discouraged. What would the transplant team decide based upon my evaluation? I had told Cathy that I was willing to eat more for the sake of being able to donate to Ryan. In fact, the very next day, I increased the amount that I ate for breakfast and lunch. I normally do not eat much early in the day, but eat a lot in the evening. Therefore, I decided to try to spread out what I had been eating more throughout the day, as well as to increase the amount. I was hoping that if the transplant team knew that I was trying to eat more, they would okay me as Ryan's donor. He was desperately needing another liver soon, and I wanted to be able to help him and his family.

But ironically, just a few days after increasing the amount that I was eating, I got the flu, along with Jubal and Joram. *Now how could I prove that I was willing to eat more?* I wondered. But I did not need to worry; the transplant team never requested any report about how much I was eating. They did develop a plan for me, however. Mimi called me on the Wednesday that I still had the flu. The doctors wanted me to meet with a counselor while I would be in Pittsburgh for the transplant and also have a dietician visit me while I was in the hospital. (At the time, I did not understand that I was supposed to meet with two separate individuals. I thought that I was going to meet with a counselor who would also give me advice about what and how much I should eat.) But Mimi also told me that the cost for the counselor would not be covered under the transplant insurance. She was going to try to arrange some financial aid for me. Unfortunately, she called the next day to inform me that she had been unable to locate any financial help. She hoped to pursue another avenue, however. I then told Mimi that I had already been offered financial help. My mother-in-law had been given some extra money that she wanted to share with me. Dawn also assured me that I could use some of the proceeds from a benefit dinner being held for Ryan's transplant that Saturday. Mimi then concluded, "As far as I am concerned then, you are the donor for Ryan." Wow! Praise the Lord; I finally had the definite answer that I could be the donor. And although I had been frustrated during the uncertain period of waiting for the transplant team's decision of whether or not I could be a donor, I had to appreciate their concern for my own health and their willingness to make special arrangements to help protect me from any possible problem due to my eating disorder.

I was, however, still concerned about the counseling that I was scheduled to have. What would the counselor be like? Would she recommend that I eat the kind of food that I considered healthy? Even though I had been promised financial aid, would there be enough money to cover the visits I would need? (Mimi did not know how many visits I would have.) I finally thought of an idea that somewhat eased my worries. I know an herbalist from Jamestown, New York, whom I highly respect. Faith, the herbalist, readily agreed to help me and even graciously offered not to charge me for visits. Pittsburgh gave their assent for Faith to do some of the follow-up sessions with me.

When I received the informational package from the hospital that detailed what I should expect for the transplant surgery, I became concerned about another issue. For the first time I was made aware that the gall bladder is always removed from a liver donor because of how closely it is located to the liver. I had to stop, think, and pray once again about whether or not I was still willing to make this sacrifice now that I understood that it required losing more than just a section of my liver. As I considered how much Christ had sacrificed to save me spiritually, I decided I should be willing to make this sacrifice to save Ryan's physical life. I did do some research about the affects of losing your gall bladder. Most sources concluded that there would be little or no affect. I asked Faith for her opinion. She told me, "I would not normally recommend a person to have his gall bladder removed, but in your case, I would definitely say to go ahead." Since she was going to be following up with me after the surgery, I felt relieved that she could give advice as needed of what I could do to help my body adjust to having no gall bladder.

Dawn and I had other serious family issues with which to deal during all the pre-transplant concerns and preparations. Dawn informed me that one of her parents had brain cancer shortly before I found out the results of Candy's tests. Following Candy's ultrasound, her doctor had ordered a DNC scraping for her. I took Candy to a gynecologist for the scraping the day after my evaluation at the eating disorder clinic. The following week the gynecologist office called and scheduled an appointment for Monday, May 11, to discuss the results of the scraping. Concerned that there might be something seriously wrong with Candy and knowing that my transplant surgery was scheduled for the nineteenth, I tried to find out information sooner than the eleventh, but the doctor was not available. When the doctor entered the waiting room to talk to Candy and me on the eleventh, he said, "You need to listen carefully. What I have to say is very serious!" He then gently broke the news that Candy had uterine cancer. He said that fortunately her cancer was in stage one and therefore he was very hopeful that he could get it all through surgery. I took this announcement rather calmly at first. But I did inform the doctor that I was about to have the transplant surgery and had been counting on Candy's help after the surgery. The doctor said that we could schedule her surgery about a month after mine. He would be waiting as long as he dared for Candy's surgery, but it would give me some time to recover.

It was not until after I left the doctor's office that reality hit, and I became very upset. Prior to this visit, I had been trying to convince myself that after all God had brought us through without closing the door to the transplant surgery, He would not allow any major concern with Candy's health to interfere. Was He finally closing the door? I did not know how all could work out with both Candy and me laid up at home, especially with a two-year-old. When I asked Jeff if I should still pursue the transplant, he said without any hesitation, "yes." I spent most of the rest of that day crying and being angry at God for allowing this crisis at this time. How could any good come out of this? Now I would have to spend this week scheduling appointments and making plans for Candy. I had already had enough to do planning for **my** surgery next week, and I did not want to get overly tired and risk getting sick the week before the surgery, especially if it caused the transplant to be delayed since Ryan's liver was in such poor condition. I did, however, feel that now I could better sympathize with and even encourage Dawn since we were both dealing with the news of a close relative having cancer.

By the next day, I felt calmer. God granted me extra strength and wisdom to make plans for Candy's surgery as well as mine. During Candy's first appointment with the gynecologist, I had met my friend Shelly, the same one who had arranged for the newspaper article about my burn to be written, coming out of an appointment while Candy was going in. Two days before I found out that Candy did indeed have cancer, I saw Shelly again at the benefit dinner for Ryan. When I shared with Shelly that Candy might have a serious health issue, she offered to help with transportation if Candy required any doctor appointments while I was still under driving restrictions following my surgery. Once it was confirmed that Candy did have cancer, I called Shelley right away to ask if she would be available to take Candy to the hospital for her hysterectomy. (Since Candy's surgery was scheduled for June 15, I might still be on driving restriction.) She agreed to help barring any schedule conflict (she has a large family). Before leaving for Pittsburgh, I was also able to arrange drivers for Candy's pre-operation appointments and any extra help I might need following Candy's operation.

The challenges before the transplant were not yet over. The same day that we learned about Candy's cancer, only a week before the transplant, I started to get a cold. Jubal and Joram had caught a cold the previous week after we three all had had the flu. I was mostly concerned about Joram who had seemed especially sick. With all the sickness he had been having lately and all the other problems that had recently arisen, I became paranoid that he too had some serious health issue. So Tuesday, the day after the discouraging news about Candy's cancer, I took Joram to my chiropractor Earl, who had been very helpful when Joram had previously been ill. He adjusted Joram, and said that his sickness appeared largely due to teething. Joram did start to improve after that visit. I was relieved!

Wednesday I found out more unfortunate news—my brother Dan's wife, Deb Lyon, just found out that her breast cancer had returned. Although I had no responsibility regarding her care since they live five hours away in Clarks Summit, Pennsylvania, this news only intensified my already stressful week. I had hoped to not overexert myself during this final week before surgery. But this week was packed with unexpected, stressful events, and I struggled with a sore throat all week, no matter what I did to relieve it.

Now why would God allow all these extra challenges just before I was going to make the greatest sacrifice thus far of my life? Wouldn't He want me to be in the best condition and frame of mind to be able to endure the physical challenges related to the sacrifice? If God truly wanted me to give to help Ryan, why had He not blessed my desire to serve Him and a needy little child with more positive confirmation while preparing for the transplant? Instead there had been some kind of obstacle to overcome all along the journey to the transplant day. Do I know why all these problems occurred? No, but if you decide to serve God in some special ministry expect many challenges even before you start your demanding ministry! Perhaps God allows Satan to send you trials when he knows you want to serve God to try to stop you. Or maybe God is testing the genuineness of your commitment to serve Him. The disciples thought they were genuine when they insisted that they would not deny Jesus even if it meant death, but when the pressure was truly on, they all forsook Him (see Matthew 26:35 and 56). God may simply be trying to strengthen your faith in Him prior to your ministry to help you better endure the rigor of service. Or God may be working on an area of your life that needs changing before you can begin your ministry, such as improving my eating habits in my case. Sometimes God is actually closing the door to a ministry. In spite of all the problems I had faced during the pre-transplant period, God had not permanently shut the door, and I believed I should pursue this service until God clearly said "no." Gradually God did begin to send miraculous signs saying "go on."

For example, the benefit dinner given for the transplant was a huge success, bringing in at least ten thousand dollars! Ryan's family and I were overwhelmed with the kindness shown to us by the hundreds of people who came to the dinner! Also God miraculously provided **free** housing for **everyone** who would be in Pittsburgh for the transplant. Scott, the husband of Jeff's sister Shari, has a cousin who lives in Swissvale, a borough of Pittsburgh. Randy, the cousin, owns a large three-story house, directly across from his own home, that he graciously offered us. It had sufficient room to comfortably house my family, Ryan's family, and friends who came to help. It was located in a friendly neighborhood, had a large back driveway where the kids could play, and was conveniently within walking distance of a grocery store and Laundromat. The house was about halfway between the children's hospital and Montefiore Hospital, where I would be. (The children's hospital had been located nearby Montefiore. But in the beginning of May, the children's hospital was moved into a nicer, larger facility partway across town. Ryan, who was in the hospital in Pittsburgh during the move from the old hospital to the new one, had the memorable opportunity to be the twenty-fifth patient transported via ambulance to the new hospital. Although it was less convenient for our families to have the hospitals farther apart, the new children's hospital was much more cheerful and provided a more comfortable place for family to stay.)

We would not have been able to successfully proceed with the transplant without the help of numerous people in many various ways. I will only name a few individuals that helped us. But both Ryan's family and mine are truly grateful to all those who gave in some way to help make the transplant possible.

As mentioned earlier, I was first inspired to consider being a living donor when I was looking for a way to give back to the community after so many people had helped my family following my accident. But I also wanted to show my gratitude to my Saviour, Who gave Himself to save me from eternal death in hell, by giving in a much smaller way to save someone from physical death. When others talked to me about my gift to Ryan, I tried to take that opportunity to tell them about Christ's incredible sacrifice for me. I prayed that someone who heard my testimony would also want to receive the gift of eternal life through Jesus Christ. Whether or not any who heard also received this gift, I may not know until eternity.

Saturday, May 16, God blessed me with an extra final gift before leaving the next day for Pittsburgh for the big surgery. As mentioned earlier, I had been struggling all that final week with a sore throat. Originally, I had intended to run my final race that Saturday before being laid up for an undetermined amount of time following the transplant. I had wanted to do it as a final fun event for Jubal and Joram too since there were special children's races scheduled. But since my throat was still quite sore on Friday, I thought that perhaps I would be wise not to run the race and possibly risk wearing myself down too much to do the surgery. But when my throat felt better on Saturday, and Jubal informed me of how much he wanted to run his race (he had been practicing that week), I decided to go to the race. Besides, I was eager to see my running companions and friends one last time before the surgery. God blessed me with allowing me to run a very good race, delight in watching Jubal and Joram run, and relish some last moments with my friends. And I did not get any sicker! *Thank You, God, for Your extra little grace shown to me!*

Chapter 3

The Sacrifice

The next day, Sunday, May 17, two days before the surgery, Ryan's family and I headed to Pittsburgh. I rode with Pete and Ryan, while Dawn and Taylor rode with Dawn's friend, Kathleen. Jeff, Jubal, Joram, and Candy were going to go down with Grandpa and Grandma Samuelson on Monday night. (Judah stayed home during the week to continue attending school and to help care for the animals. After finishing the chores on Monday and Tuesday evening, Judah spent the night with his friend Nate since no one else was home.)

At 9:00 A.M. Monday, I met with Jennie the psychotherapist chosen by the transplant team for me. I was very comfortable and impressed with the psychotherapist. But I was surprised when I asked her about some dietary guidelines that she told me to discuss those questions with the dietician. *Dietician? What dietician?* I thought. As mentioned earlier, when Mimi had informed me that the doctors decided to allow me to be a living donor if I agreed to counseling, I had not understood that I was to meet with two separate people—a counselor and a dietician. But I was relieved once I found out that I did not need to pay for the dietician's services because, as a member of the UPMC dietary staff, she would simply meet with me during my hospital stay. I also was grateful that the therapist charged less than the first cost quoted to me.

Following my meeting with the therapist, at 10:00 A.M. I met with Mimi and my surgeon, Dr. Humar—they briefly reviewed all the pre-operation regulations and when and where I needed to go for the surgery the following morning.

While waiting for my family to arrive, I enjoyed the afternoon with Dawn's friend, Kathleen, and Taylor. Kathleen went shopping for goodies such as curtains and small bathroom wastebaskets to help make the house more "homey." She also graciously offered to pamper me prior to my surgery by paying for me to have a pedicure. Never having had one before, I was at first thrilled to accept the kind offer. Then I remembered that I would have to decline the offer since I was not allowed to have on any polish during the surgery. I did enjoy getting to know Kathleen better, chatting with her while she and Taylor received a pedicure. I also watched with fascination the diligent, detailed Chinese workers beautify others' feet.

When my family arrived, I had an unexpected pleasant surprise! My friend Susan Bauer had also come along. She told me, "I was worried about you and had to come down to see you." We didn't know how helpful her presence would be. Grandma Samuelson called her an "angel." I had planned on Candy and Grandma watching Jubal and Joram while Jeff was with me for the surgery. Candy and Grandma were very helpful, but they needed young, spry Susan who could better keep up with an active six- and two-year old. Susan had also brought along her daughter Emily, only three days younger than Jubal, who was great company for my boys. Susan literally became like a second mother to my boys during and after my surgery. Joram even at times called her "mommy." He still will ask for Susan often when he is sad or bored.

Monday night I went to bed uneasy. I worried that the hospital might postpone the surgery due to the sore throat I still had. But Jeff told me, "Just go to sleep." (While preregistering earlier that day over the phone for surgery, I learned that I should have discontinued the use of all vitamins and herbs five days before the surgery. I considered it God's providence that I had not received this information earlier because I had needed extra natural supplements to deal with my sore throat and had been advised to take specific supplements to help prevent the development of any infection after the surgery.)

Grandpa Samuelson dropped Jeff and me off at Montefiore Hospital at 5:00 A.M. Tuesday. Ryan had already been admitted to the children's hospital on Monday. Since Ryan was in one hospital and I was in another partway across town, the liver section removed from me would be first cleaned, then placed in a sterile cooler, and finally transported to the children's hospital via ambulance. The transportation time takes about twenty minutes.

Once at the hospital, I began to get a little nervous, but found relief by quoting Psalm 34, especially the following verses: verse 4, "I sought the LORD, and He heard me, And delivered me from all my fears," and verse 7, "the angel of the LORD encamps all around those who fear Him, And delivers them." The last thing that I remember before the surgery was the anesthesiologist asking while wheeling me in a stretcher down the hall, "Do you feel sleepy yet?" I said, "no," needlessly worried about not being totally unconscious for the surgery.

My time in ICU, Tuesday evening through Wednesday, was mostly a blur. I vaguely remember Jeff visiting me after the surgery. He said, "you look good," but I **felt** terrible! I was grateful when Jeff told me that because my liver was bigger than the doctor had expected, he only took twenty-five percent of it, not forty-five percent as he had originally intended. I remember asking myself, *What have I done?* and feeling as though I literally wanted to die. Wednesday morning Jeff and the boys came in to say "good by" before they went home until the weekend. I was deeply moved when I saw tears in Jeff's eyes! Joram was struggling to get out of Daddy's arms—not to see Mommy, but to check out all the interesting hospital equipment. After Jeff and the boys left, Candy and Susan came in. Candy also was crying and wanted to hug me, but I had to tell her "no" due to my pain and discomfort.

I remember looking at the clock later that day. It said 2:15, but I was sure that it actually was about 7:00 P.M. because it had seemed like such a long day. I asked my nurse, Emily, if the clock had stopped. She answered, "No, you just really lose track of time while in ICU." That evening they prepared to move me from ICU to twelfth floor. Emily and a male nurse rolled up my sheet, lifted me up, and then laid me onto the stretcher. The moment I landed on the stretcher may have been the most painful second of my life. I groaned loudly and wanted to scream out with my whole body! I felt as though my whole insides had been slammed against the wall and then just plopped to the floor. I wondered how I could endure the move from the stretcher to the bed in my new room upstairs. All I could do was frantically pray. I vigilantly watched every movement of the nurse pulling the stretcher, terrified that she would hit something. She appeared to just barely miss the walls and everything that we passed! But we safely reached room seventy-eight of the twelfth floor. To my great relief, Emily suggested to the other nurses, "Although she is not heavy, I think we should use the moving board to slide her onto the bed. She was really hurt when we moved her to the stretcher." Wow! The moving board made the second move barely painful, so different from the first move! I silently praised the Lord!

During Wednesday night, the PCT (personal care technician) told me that they would be getting me up to walk on Thursday. I could not imagine at the time getting up yet! But when my catheter was removed in the morning, I knew that eventually I would have to get up. Some nurses were preparing to get me up when they had to leave for another more urgent need. Dreading the pain that I supposed I would have when I got up, I was temporarily relieved. Having barely changed position since the operation and knowing that I would have to get up soon, I decided to try moving around a little on my own. I was encouraged when I was able to move with less pain than I had anticipated. Therefore, when I needed to use the restroom shortly after moving around, I was less afraid to get up. I pushed my call button for help. Two nurses/ PCT's helped me get up, and I did fine! I felt well enough to get up three or four more times that day, and even took a slow, short walk in the hallways with aid. I was so grateful to be feeling well enough to be up walking again!

While Grandpa Samuelson was visiting me that afternoon, a woman came in with a webcam to allow Ryan and me to see one another and chat. Since this was only the second time that the UPMC hospital system had used this new device, the woman was still unsure of how to properly work the webcam. Ryan and I could hear one another, but we could not see each other very clearly. Although I actually was feeling too lousy to communicate much with Ryan at the time, I was still glad to have some contact with him and pleased to be one of the first set of patients to use the hospital system's new webcam.

The next morning, Friday, Dr. Humar asked me, "So when do you want to go home?" Originally I was informed that the average hospital stay time after a liver donation is seven days. Shortly before my operation Mimi told me about a lady who had been released after only five days. Obviously, Dr. Humar thought that I too would be well enough to leave after five days. I, however, gave him no definite answer at the time because I did not feel as though I would be ready to leave the next day.

The dietician came to see me that same morning. While she was giving me guidelines for how much I should eat, she suddenly realized how odd it sounded for her to be telling me to increase my daily food portions when I had had nothing to eat except Jell-o and clear liquids since Monday night. I had been amused thinking this same thing. But I was looking forward to lunch when I would have my first solid food since the surgery. Although concerned about how well my body would adjust once I started to eat again, I did well eating balanced meals as long as I ate smaller, more frequent meals and did not eat too fast. I was also relieved that I did not notice any difficulty with eating related to no longer having a gall bladder.

Friday, I was thrilled to have a student nurse tell me that she had heard I am a runner and she is too. I do not know how she found out that I am a runner, but I certainly enjoyed sharing about our common hobby. She had recently run the half-marathon during Pittsburgh's marathon. Pete, who had been with Ryan in the hospital at the time, had earlier told me that he was able to watch some of that race. Friday night, I was again delighted to have another student nurse take time to discuss running with me. He too had somehow found out that I run, and he used to also be a runner. He was currently biking competively rather than running due to struggling with shin splints while running. Saturday morning, assuring me that I would be released that day, he came in to say "good by" and "keep running." I greatly appreciated the personal interest and attention shown me from these two student nurses!

Saturday morning, a doctor told me that I could go home that day. I had mixed emotions—hesitation about whether I felt well enough to leave yet, but excitement to get out also. Taking a shower and putting on a comfortable pair of pajamas helped me feel better. I had been looking forward all week to getting out of the uncomfortable hospital gown and into those adorable pajamas that Susan had thoughtfully given me for this occasion.

I had to retain a Jackson-Pratt (JP) bulb attached to my stomach drainage tube for a few more days. The JP bulb is often used following such surgeries as abdominal to suction out extra body fluid, helping to prevent infection and promote faster healing. I called the bulb my "constant companion" or "sidekick" since I was always aware of its bulky presence at my side. The large bulb I had while in the hospital was bigger than had been previously used at Montefiore, and even some of the hospital staff had expressed amazement over its immensity. I had hoped to have my sidekick removed upon discharge since it was a nuisance, always getting in my way. To my great relief, before my discharge, the inconveniently large bulb was replaced by a smaller bulb.

Chapter 4

Discouragement and Hope

As I was preparing to leave the hospital, I reflected upon my many blessings. After all the challenges along the way to the actual transplant, I had been able to give to Ryan. I had come through the surgery safely and was able to leave the hospital after a very short stay. I had received excellent care while in the hospital, and I appreciated the transplant team's extra effort prior to the surgery to provide me with specific guidance toward eating sufficiently for a full recovery. But I was discouraged about the reports I had received concerning Ryan. Of course, my desire when I chose to donate to Ryan was for his body not to reject the liver, for him to heal quickly, for his intense suffering to be minimized, and finally for him to be able to enjoy a more normal childhood. For example, I was hoping that he would be able to play more freely with Jubal, who is only a year younger. But although I was told that the liver itself seemed to be working fine, Ryan was not responding well overall. I just kept hoping and praying for his full, speedy recovery.

Dave, Jeff's youngest brother, and Grandpa Samuelson picked me up from the hospital. As soon as I stepped into the sunshine and fresh air I felt better and for the first time felt as though I was truly well enough to leave the hospital. My journey from the hospital was a little nerve racking because I was worried that any little bump or pothole would jar my stomach and hurt. But Dave successfully drove me to the house in Swissvale without causing me any discomfort. When we arrived at the house, balloons flying from the porch greeted me. Susan had come back down with both her daughters, Samantha and Emily. She had also brought with her Jubal, Joram, Grandma Samuelson, and Candy. (Grandpa Samuelson had stayed in Swissvale all week to help. Jeff, along with Judah, joined us later Saturday evening.) The always thoughtful

Susan had brought a helium tank, filled balloons, and hung them up to welcome me. I was relieved to hear how well the boys had been doing without Mommy. Friday, Susan had taken them to Midway, a children's amusement park about twenty minutes from our home. The boys had had a fantastic time, but I think Joram wore out Susan, repeatedly dragging her up the stairs of a large slide for another exhilarating ride down.

I was pleased that I was able to walk around better than I had expected, but I was concerned about how I would sleep. A bed had been set up for me on the first floor so that I did not need to go up and down the stairs, although going up and down the stairs was not too strenuous for me. The challenge that I was facing was how to lie comfortably on a flat bed. Jeff tried to help me find a comfortable position in bed my first night out of the hospital, but lying on a flat bed was too painful. I told Jeff that I wished I had a recliner. Jeff began to search the large house for a possible recliner. Just then, Randy, the owner, walked in. Dave asked him if he had a recliner. He said, "yes," and he, along with Jeff and Dave, went to get it. Only about ten minutes after my unsuccessful attempt to lie down in bed and my desperate desire for a recliner, I had one! God heard my plea for help and graciously responded immediately! I told Randy he was an "angel" sent from God at just the right moment. (He and his wife, Karen, had already been a big blessing to us through allowing us to use their house and by providing some delicious meals from their own local restaurant to those staying at the house.) The recliner made sleep possible, although I could only sleep for about two hours at a time before having to get up, due to stiffness and discomfort.

After taking Jubal and Joram to a children's museum Sunday afternoon, Susan had to return to New York. I needed to remain in the Pittsburgh area for another week to be near Montefiore Hospital in case if any problems arose. Jubal and Joram were going to stay with me so that I could continue Jubal's home schooling and to free Jeff and Candy to go back to work that week. Since the following day was Memorial Day, Jeff, Candy, and Judah stayed for the holiday. Fortunately, I would not be left without help for the boys after my family returned home. My niece Katie, who had arrived from Virginia while I was still in the hospital, along with her mom Shari, Jeff's sister, who arrived Sunday evening after Susan left, would be available to help care for the boys and Taylor. Jeff's parents both stayed for the week, being flexible to help wherever needed, whether at the house or at the children's hospital. Pete and Dawn were still spending most of their time with Ryan at the hospital. It was such a blessing to see how God always provided the people we needed to help.

Sunday evening, I went to see Ryan for the first time since our surgeries. Unfortunately, he still was not feeling well enough to respond much. Pete took me down the hall to visit another lady who was scheduled to donate part of her liver to her daughter later that week. She asked me questions of what she should expect and how she could be better prepared. I was glad to share what I had experienced through my surgery, hoping that she would benefit from my information and experience.

On Memorial Day, Grandma Samuelson, who had grown up in Edgewood, a close community to Pittsburgh, excitedly took us to visit her childhood school's outdoor sports training area and then to see her former home. Jeff, Judah, and Candy headed back home that afternoon.

On Tuesday, I had another visit with Jennie and then with Mimi and Dr. Humar. They were all pleased with how well I looked and was moving about; and, to my great relief, the doctor pulled my JP! I was also grateful that I had only needed a few pain pills after leaving the hospital, and I took my very last one, which was actually only half a pill, on Wednesday morning. I felt well enough to do a lot more activities than I had expected I would be able to do. I even went to a children's museum with my boys, Shari, Katie, Grandma, and Taylor—I strolled around the museum very cautiously and sat down frequently. Since it was Grandma's birthday that Friday, we had a surprise birthday party for her Thursday night. At Taylor's suggestion, we had fun decorating for a luau party. I even enjoyed plodding carefully to the nearby store with Taylor, Katie, and Shari to pick up some decorations and gifts for Grandma. Friday, the doctor gave me permission to go home! I was very happy with my fast progress, but still disappointed about Ryan. I had hoped for some encouraging news about him before I went home, but he still was not showing much, if any improvement.

My good friend Pam prepared a delicious meal for my family the day I returned home. It was a blessing not to have to worry about a meal for that first evening home. To my relief, I found that I was able to do most of the work around the house except anything that required lifting over ten pounds. Since I could not lift over ten pounds for about six weeks, I greatly appreciated the home school young people who voluntarily came over during the day to help me with jobs such as carrying laundry, vacuuming, or picking up Joram. Both Jubal and Joram enjoyed having other young people around, even though they were somewhat older. I am very grateful to Liz Nixon for willingly coordinating who would come and on what days.

For about a week I did well and was steadily getting stronger. But then one day, when my German Shepherd Sasha started to run after some other dogs, I instinctively reached out to grab her leash. When she lunged forward, I cried out in pain, having wrenched my incision area. Since the pain increased over the next few days, I became concerned that I might have a hernia. Therefore, when I took Candy for her pre-operation appointment with our primary physician, Natalie, I asked Natalie to also examine me. I was very relieved when she informed me that it was not a hernia. "Take it extra easy for a few days, and avoid hills during your walks until you feel better," she instructed me.

The location of our house posed another challenge—how to avoid walking up a hill. We live at a four-corner intersection where Steinhoff Road meets Carpenter Pringle Road. Our driveway makes up the fourth section. If I were to turn right from our driveway onto Carpenter Pringle Road or go straight ahead onto Steinhoff, I would immediately head down hill. Although both these hills are small, they present a challenging finish to a rigorous walk or run. Furthermore, whether turning right or left onto Carpenter Pringle Road or going straight onto Steinhoff, I would encounter a larger hill within half a mile of my house. I decided to walk a distance of about half a mile on Carpenter Pringle Road, since that route included only the smallest of all the hills, and walked this route several times daily to maintain my three-mile walk routine. I managed this boring, but still productive walk, without any problem, and soon was well enough to once again walk a three-mile distance anywhere I wanted around my home area.

Candy's hysterectomy surgery was scheduled for June 15. I had needed others to drive Candy and me to her pre-operation appointments. I was allowed to drive by the weekend just prior to her surgery. Therefore, I was able to drive Candy and me to her surgery, stay at the hospital during her surgery, and then drive home myself following the surgery. As I sat with Candy during her pre-surgery routines, I was finally able to appreciate some benefits of her requiring major surgery so soon following mine. First, she had enjoyed the attention she received from others who learned about her surgery while they discussed mine with me. Second, I was better able to help prepare Candy for the procedures she would experience during her surgery and recovery since I had just undergone many of the same situations during the transplant. Third, her preoccupation with my surgery and needs helped keep her mind off her own upcoming surgery. Fourth, observing how quickly and well I was recovering provided Candy encouragement that she too could have a quick and successful recovery.

I was greatly relieved and pleased with how calm Candy appeared while waiting in the pre-operation area. A few hours later, I had to truly praise the Lord when the doctor came out to report that Candy's surgery had gone well, and it appeared that they had been able to get all of the cancer. Candy went on to recover very well from the surgery, and follow-ups verified that her cancer was indeed gone! We also managed around the home better than I thought possible with two of us unable to lift much, especially with a two-year-old wanting our attention. I learned to do most of the household chores without lifting too much at once. Jubal became a big help during the day, even picking up Joram for brief moments. Also, since Joram still slept in Jeff's and my bedroom, I would push Joram's crib over to our bed for him to climb onto our bed and then crawl into his crib. When he needed to get out of bed, he would crawl out of his crib onto our bed and slide off. Also if needed, I could still call upon home schoolers to help.

My one-month checkup in Pittsburgh went well. The doctor was pleased with my progress. But I was disappointed with his response when I asked him how soon I would be able to start running again. I assumed that he might say that I could start running again in three to four months after the surgery. Instead he said, "You may start running again after six months." I thought, *Oh no! How can I wait that long?* I hoped that I would get a second opinion from another doctor since this doctor was not the head doctor of the transplant team and was also the same one who had told me during my one-week checkup that I could not drive for several weeks after my surgery. He promptly reduced the driving restriction period to two weeks after Mimi told him that normally liver donors were permitted to drive two weeks following their surgery. But there was no second opinion given concerning the running restriction period. I resolved, therefore, to accept this long restriction from my favorite hobby as another minor challenge that God would help me endure for the sake of being able to help save Ryan's life. And God did faithfully take me through this challenge. I learned to be a very fast walker, even participating in area walk races and winning every one I did. I count this honor as God's grace and blessing to me for my obedience in this small area of waiting to run.

Unfortunately, Ryan did not have the same good report as Candy and I had had following our surgeries. Two days after Candy's successful surgery, we received very discouraging news about Ryan. Wednesday, June 17, Pete called to tell us that the kidney which he had donated to Ryan three years earlier had now failed. Pete was obviously devastated! I was also discouraged because I felt like my sacrifice, hopes, and prayers had been to no avail. It appeared that Ryan would need another kidney transplant. The doctors even considered doing another liver transplant at the same time as the kidney so that both organs would be from the same source, thus hopefully reducing the possibility of one organ being rejected while the body was trying to accept the other organ from a different source. I had to remind myself that I did help prolong Ryan's life because he could not have survived much longer with his green, hardened, useless liver. I prayed for a miraculous healing of his current kidney. Grandma Samuelson did call on June 24, to tell us that the kidney was producing some urine again. Somewhat encouraged, my family hoped and prayed all summer that the kidney would continue to improve. But it did not.

Chapter 5

Perseverance

In the meantime, Ryan had other health issues. After being baffled for weeks by all the problems Ryan was having following the liver transplant, the doctors finally concluded that he had developed the small-for-size liver syndrome (SFSS). Unfortunately, the portion size of the liver grafted from me to him was actually smaller than he initially needed. Determining the correct size liver mass needed for a recipient still requires more research and experience. Although SSFS can cause some serious health conditions such as infections and congestion of the liver, fortunately, these health issues are usually resolved as the donated liver grows. Finally, around the first of September, Ryan was released from Children's Hospital of Pittsburgh. At first, he stayed at the house in Swissvale because he required therapy for relearning to walk after being laid up in bed for months and dialysis. Eventually he was able to come home to New York for weekend visits. Once he returned home permanently, he began traveling to Buffalo three times a week for dialysis while awaiting another kidney transplant.

One other major challenging event hit all of the Samuelson family shortly before the end of 2009. On the first of December, Jeff's father had a major stoke; and on December 11, 2009, Phil Samuelson passed away. There are two blessings for which we were very grateful in the midst of our sorrow. One is that Grandpa Samuelson was happy to fulfill a very important ministry the summer before he died, not knowing that it would be his final main service to others. Remaining in Pittsburgh for most of Ryan's hospitalization, he was able to transport people to and from Montefiore or the children's hospital and was willing to sit patiently at either hospital until he was needed to transport someone, pass on a message to the rest of the family, or run some other necessary errand. No longer having any pressing responsibilities at his home in New York, Grandpa was the ideal person to remain in Pittsburgh to help as needed. Ryan also dearly loved his Grandpa and was encouraged by his close presence. The other blessing, which greatly encouraged Jeff, is that God gave Jeff one final opportunity to talk to his father about his relationship with Jesus Christ following the stroke. One night while Jeff was staying with his father in the hospital, his dad suddenly became more alert than he had been or would be again. Jeff, therefore, took that moment to ask his father, "Have you repented of your sin and asked Jesus to be your Saviour? Do you know for sure that you are going to heaven?" His father nodded his headed vigorously "yes," intensely squeezing Jeff's hand. Relieved, Jeff wept with joy!

Although the passing of his Grandpa Samuelson added sorrow to Ryan's suffering, he is still surrounded by many people who love him and want to see him heal. Why did God allow a little boy to continue suffering after two people who loved him gave to safe his life and help reduce his pain? Why did God allow me to finally be able to donate to Ryan after overcoming numerous obstacles, only to have him require another transplant so soon? I do not know. Part of the challenge of making a sacrifice is to be willing to make the sacrifice, not knowing the consequence. Jesus willingly made the biggest sacrifice of all, **knowing** that the majority of those for whom He died would reject Him. Also God can use suffering for our own good and to bring Himself glory. And while we continue to pray for Ryan's healing, we are very grateful for the many times that God has brought him through past crises and trust Him to continue to perform more miracles in this precious little boy's life.

My final challenge to all believers who read this, and to myself, is never stop being willing to make whatever sacrifice God calls us to make, no matter the challenges that accompany the sacrifice. May God help us to be able to say along with Paul, ". . . we also glory in tribulations, knowing that tribulation produces perseverance; and perseverance, character; and character, hope. Now hope does not disappoint, because the love of God has been poured out in our hearts by the Holy Spirit who was given to us," Romans 5:3-5. And if you have not yet experienced God's outpouring of His love in your heart by receiving Jesus Christ as your own personal Saviour from sin and its horrendous consequences, my hope and prayer is that you will very soon!

On Wednesday, May 19, 2010, we celebrated the one-year anniversary of Ryan's liver transplant. He looked great and had grown significantly taller over the past year. After a delicious cookout held in Ryan's backyard, I stood observing the children playing tag. My heart was overwhelmed with joy and deep satisfaction as I watched Ryan run and laugh along with all the other children. Yes, indeed, the sacrifice, even with all its challenges, had been worth it!

Picture from newspaper story regarding Jubal's birth

Judah, Lydia, Jubal, and Jeffrey Samuelson
(courtesy of the Jamestown, New York *Post-Journal*)

Samuelson family a year following the liver transplant

Lydia, Judah (standing); Jubal, Jeffrey, and Joram (sitting) Samuelson
(photographer Pam Gaeta)

Ryan Samuelson in Children's Hospital of Pittsburgh prior to his liver transplant

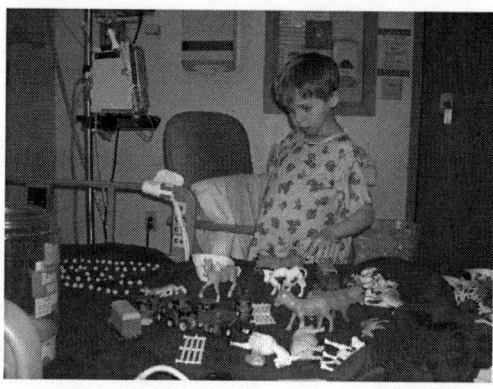

Ryan Samuelson with his calf Rose the winter following his transplant

Ryan's family at his home the autumn following his transplant

Dawn, Taylor, Peter, and Ryan Samuelson

The Author

Lydia Ann Samuelson grew up on a dairy farm in southwestern New York surrounded by luscious, rolling meadows bordered with stately hardwood forests. Never tiring of the lovely view facing her home, Lydia does not regret still living on the old family homestead with her husband, Jeffrey; three sons, Judah, Jubal, and Joram; and an older sister, Candy Lyon. Chickens have now replaced dairy cows as the main animal on the farm. Prior to having children, Lydia taught upper elementary for a few years at a local Christian school. Since having children, Lydia has kept busy caring for her family, home schooling her children, tutoring, serving in Christian ministries, writing, and running. Lydia desires to share the good news of Jesus Christ and to encourage other believers in their walk with Christ through her writing.

Edwards Brothers,Inc!
Thorofare, NJ 08086
29 September, 2010
BA2010272